CW00518876

Tea for the Tui

First published in 2007 by New Holland Publishers (NZ) Ltd
Auckland • Sydney • London • Cape Town
www.newhollandpublishers.co.nz

218 Lake Road, Northcote, Auckland, New Zealand
Unit 1, 66 Gibbes Street, Chatswood, NSW 2067, Australia
86–88 Edgware Road, London W2 2EA, United Kingdom
Wembley Square, First Floor, Solan Street, Gardens, Cape Town 8000, South Africa

Copyright © 2007 in text: Rosemary Tully and Mark Golley
Copyright © 2007 in illustration: Rachel Lockwood, with the exception of front cover and
    pages 9, 15 and 87 by Deborah Hinde
Copyright © 2007 New Holland Publishers (NZ) Ltd

Publishing manager: Christine Thomson
Editor: Kate Stone
Designer: Gülen Shevki-Taylor
Layout: Dee Murch
Illustration: Rachel Lockwood / Deb Hinde

National Library of New Zealand Cataloguing-in-Publication Data

Tully, Rosemary.
Tea for the tui : fun recipes to entice birds to your garden /
Rosemary Tully and Mark Golley ; illustrations by Rachel
Lockwood and Deborah Hinde. 1st ed.
Includes index.
ISBN 978-1-86966-167-0
1. Bird attracting. 2. Birds—Feeding and feeds. I. Golley, Mark.
II. Lockwood, Rachel. III. Hinde, Deborah, 1957- IV. Title.
639.978—dc 22

10 9 8 7

Reproduction by Image Centre Ltd., Auckland
Printed in China by Toppan Leefung Printing Ltd.

All rights reserved. No part of this publication may be reproduced, stored in any retrieval system
or transmitted, in any form or by any means, electronic, mechanical, photocopying, recording
or otherwise, without the prior written permission of the publishers and copyright holders.

While every care has been taken to ensure the information contained in this book is as accurate as
possible, the author and publishers can accept no responsibility for loss, damage, injury or inconvenience
sustained by any person or wildlife as a consequence of using the advice contained herein.

Tea for the Tui

Fun recipes to entice birds to your garden

Rosemary Tully

contents

Introduction

When you browse the titles in your local bookstore, you can almost hear the shelves groaning under the weight of a plethora of cookery titles. Old ways, new ways, Thai, French, Chinese, Indian and Italian. Almost every Kiwi has an Alison Holst, a Julie Biuso or Edmonds Cookery book tucked away somewhere. We seem to love cookery books and cooking for ourselves.

How often, though, have you thought about a little kitchen fun and cooking for some rather different guests?

The most frequent visitors that you can entertain with your culinary skill visit every day of the year, come rain or shine. They wait patiently for anything that you care to serve to them, they never complain and you can guarantee that they are always grateful. They may even show their appreciation with a song. No garden should be without them, as they always brighten up a dull day. 'They' are, of course, birds!

Birds are, undoubtedly, the life and colour of any garden, wherever it may be. You can live in the remotest of areas, or in the most populated; your garden can be huge, or just a few metres wide. But one thing is guaranteed: with food made available, the birds will come.

This book aims to bring you some of the most popular and successful bird food recipes there are.

So whether it's tea for a Tui, a snack for a Silvereye or a bellyful for a Blackbird, there should be plenty here to entice a variety of visitors to your bird table or bird feeders. And, hopefully, the whole family will enjoy making the recipes, and then take pleasure in the reaction of the birds! Do remember that it sometimes takes a while for the birds to find the food, so patience is needed.

The Importance of Feeding

There are numerous reasons why we should feed our wild birds. Perhaps the most obvious of all is that, without our help, many of them may die, particularly during severe winters. Smaller species such as Waxeyes, Finches and Sparrows are especially at risk because they all use up vital energy searching for food during the shorter winter days. And so, if we can help them by providing a safe and regular source of energy, then so much the better. Loss of suitable habitat has also become an issue with the natural garden being taken over by concrete, and bark and stone gardens covering up the bare earth and hiding the insects and grubs the birds like to eat. We, in turn, lose plants and insects that are vital components in a bird's food chain, particularly during the summer, when there are millions of baby birds in need of food.

You needn't confine your garden bird feeding to winter and early spring. Over the years, the question of whether to feed birds during the breeding season has been something of a 'hot potato'. Now, though, conservation organisations have recognised the benefits and importance of feeding all year round. Providing an easy source of food in the garden during the summer keeps the adults in good condition and leaves them more time to feed the growing chicks with caterpillars, insects and grubs, which they will not need to eat themselves!

For the spring and summer it is best to:

- Continue to provide food, but ensure variety at all times (perhaps including live food too).
- Avoid using whole peanuts; a wire feeder or small string bag will ensure that adults take only small pieces.
- Reduce the amount of food you put out as autumn approaches, as this is the one time of year when natural food supplies should be at their optimum.

In addition to food, you should always ensure that there is a good supply of fresh water available. Many birds need to drink at least a couple of times through the course of a day, so fresh water is invaluable. A separate source for bathing is also a welcome addition for birds in your garden.

If you want more information on this and other matters relating to the subject, why not visit the website of the Royal Forest and Bird Protection Society, www.forestandbird.org.nz? It's packed with useful tips on turning your garden into a haven for wildlife.

Good Foods, Bad Foods

Throughout the book several 'core ingredients' are used for a number of recipes. Many of them are likely to be on hand within the kitchen, but if you feel a *Tea for the Tui* meal-making frenzy coming on, it's worth ensuring that you have available the essentials listed below. I have also listed some foods you should not use, as they may be bad for a bird's health (avocado, salt, rotten food), may spread disease (honey), or may be invasive plants (kiwifruit). Where a recipe calls for a 'jar' of peanut butter, this is a regular 375–400g jar.

Good Foods	Bad Foods
• Suet (animal or vegetable)	• Avocado
• Wild bird seed mixture (or cage bird seed)	• Salt
• Unsalted peanut butter	• Kiwifruit
• Stale cornflakes or rice bubbles (or cornmeal)	• Honey (use malt instead)
• Raisins or sultanas	• Anything mouldy, rancid or rotten
• Breadcrumbs (not mouldy)	

Seeds & Pulses

All manner of seeds and pulses are available throughout the country, in specialist wholefood stores or in most super-markets. The recipes in this chapter are all incredibly simple to follow and will always prove popular with seed-eating species, such as Chaffinches, Greenfinches, and Sparrows. The first recipe doesn't even require any cooking!

Malt Twigs

You may have heard the old joke, 'What's brown and sticky?' 'A stick!'... Well here's the *Tea for the Tui* punchline – a 'Malt Twig'! This recipe takes no time at all to prepare, and the seed-eaters that pop in to the garden will be ever more likely to linger with a 'Malt Twig' on offer – they will simply love this sweet-toothed treat! Keep your eyes on those Finches and Sparrows as squabbles are likely when they begin to taste this oh-so-simple snack. Adapted from treats that are popular with aviculturalists, this easy-to-make recipe should make wild garden birds very appreciative.

Ingredients

Several sticks or twigs

Malt (may need warming to make it runnier)

Wild bird seed

Method

✎ Have a wander in your garden or local reserve, and search out as many sticks and twigs as you fancy that are an average 1–5cm in diameter. (They can be as long as you want.)

✎ Take a spoonful or two of runny malt and spread it all over the selected twigs and sticks. Now simply pour the wild bird seed mixture over the malted sticks. Once they are covered in seeds, place the sticks in the fridge to harden up and then hang them in the garden, from feeders or other twigs.

Bird Balls

This wonderfully messy concoction is one of the few recipes in the book that actually have a specific measurement! A visit to the bulk bins will set you up for most of these simple-to-find ingredients.

Ingredients

½kg lard

1 jar unsalted crunchy peanut butter

5 cups cornmeal (available in many wholefood shops) –
crushed stale cornflakes/rice bubbles make a good substitute

6 cups quick-cook porridge oats

2 cups sunflower seeds

2 cups raisins

Method

✎ Cut the lard into smallish blocks so that you can soften it sufficiently when mixing in other ingredients. Once soft enough, put the lard blocks into an old mixing bowl and add the peanut butter, cornmeal (or cereal) and porridge oats. Using your hands, mix everything together. When you are happy that all the ingredients are well mixed, divide the stodgy mess into half a dozen 'portions' and roll them into ball shapes. Finally, roll these balls into the sunflower seeds and raisins.

✎ Suspend the balls from your bird feeders inside some sturdy netting, or place the balls inside a bird feeder. Alternatively, form the balls around sturdy twine and tie them to nearby branches. Then it's time to wash up!

Nice 'n' Seedzy

As well as slaving over a hot stove for your garden bird visitors, it's nice to be able to offer them up something which takes no time at all to prepare, involves barely a bowl being offered up to the dishwasher and is incredibly nutritious too. All you need are seeds. The Finches that pay you regular visits will love this simple mixture. And, as mentioned in the Method (see opposite), you could try adapting the recipe to make seed balls too. You could also add some crushed cream crackers into the mixture as an additional nibbly treat.

Ingredients

2½ cups sunflower seeds

1 cup millet seeds

½ cup wild bird seed

Method

🖋 Pop all the seeds into a bowl, mix, and serve in a seed hopper/feeder! *Voilà*! A guaranteed hit. You can also bind the seeds together and form seed balls using suet (animal or vegetable suet is fine) and perhaps some unsalted peanut butter. A combination of both works particularly well, but melt them both down before adding the seeds. As the mixture cools, pop it into the fridge or freezer compartment to ensure the fat hardens properly.

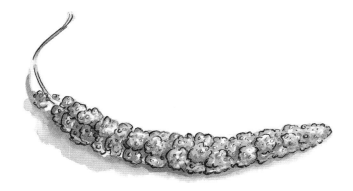

Summer Sunflower Seedheads

This is another seeds 'recipe' which needs very little attention to detail. In fact, since you can leave the kitchen out of this altogether, it's a bit cheeky to even call it a recipe! This idea should prove to be a cinch for attracting Finches.

Ingredients

Sunflower heads

Method

🖋 Many people are keen gardeners and some may also grow sunflowers. What is needed for this easy bird feeding idea is a number of seeding sunflower heads. If you don't grow your own, have a chat with a friendly florist, or even a local supermarket which sells flowers — they may have access to sunflower heads.

🖋 Cut off the sunflower heads, along with around 30–36cm of the stalk. Take a piece of strong twine (rope or tough string will suffice) and tie it securely to the stalk (you may need to tie some twine around the flower head, too). Then secure the flower head to the side of a bird table, a feeding station pole or to the branch of a tree.

Cornbread Treat

This recipe is cooked in the microwave, but you could try cooking it in the oven. Some of the birds that visit your garden will love the corn grits that are included in the mixture. You can experiment with additions like bird seed or fruit, but you may need to add more liquid.

Ingredients

1 ½ cups flour

1 heaped teaspoon baking powder

1 teaspoon baking soda

½ cup raw sugar

1 cup cornmeal

1 cup corn grits

½ cup olive oil

2 tablespoons margarine

1 cup liquid (half milk and water)

1 egg

Method

✒ In a bowl, mix all the dry ingredients together. In another bowl, mix all the liquids together. Add liquid to dry ingredients. Line a microwave dish with plastic wrap (or just grease the dish). Pour in the mixture. Cook on High in the microwave for 8 minutes. Check with a toothpick to see if the centre of the cornbread is cooked. Allow more cooking time if it is needed.

✒ Once baked, allow the bread to cool before cutting into reasonable-sized pieces. Freeze any pieces that you don't use and defrost them when required. Crumble the slices before putting them out onto your bird table.

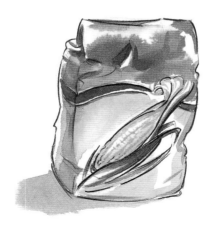

Beans & Rice

Although this is one of the more time-consuming recipes featured in *Tea for the Tui*, it is extremely rewarding. Full of goodness and nutritionally sound, 'Beans & Rice' should be a hit with Thrushes and Blackbirds, especially in wintertime. The beans and lentils used here are widely available in many wholefood stores and supermarkets.

Ingredients

¼ cup dried pinto beans	¼ cup dried lentils
¼ cup dried kidney beans	1 large chopped carrot
¼ cup dried butter beans	1 cup cooked brown rice
¼ cup dried haricot beans	1 cup cooked white rice
¼ cup dried split peas	1 cup sweetcorn

Method

✒ Soak all of the beans, peas and lentils in a pan overnight before cooking. When you have done this, drain them and rinse with cold water. Then refill the pan with water before adding the carrot. Slowly cook the beans and carrot on a low heat for around an hour.

✒ Add the pre-cooked rice, along with the sweetcorn. Cook the mixture until the rice and corn are warmed through. Allow the 'Beans & Rice' mixture to cool down thoroughly before putting it out onto the bird table. You may choose to put the mixture into a container before putting it outside.

✒ Any 'Beans & Rice' mixture that is left can be put into the freezer – just remember to thaw it out before giving it to the birds!

Bean Soup

A variation on the previous recipe that also proves popular with a number of garden bird species; bursting with protein and just as easy to prepare as 'Beans & Rice', 'Bean Soup' ought to be given an avian nod of approval. Thrushes will be more than happy to step up to the bird table for some of this, and try getting the Starlings to stay away! As mentioned in the recipe itself, there are plenty of alternatives you could consider using, so why not experiment and come up with your own version.

Ingredients

1 bag dried vegetable and pasta mixture (available in most supermarkets and contains peas, beans, pearl barley, etc.) – as an alternative, use as many varieties of pulses as your cupboard can run to

1 cup uncooked brown rice

1 bag frozen sweetcorn

Method

🖋 Follow the instructions on the packet – a vegetable and pasta mixture usually takes around 50 minutes to cook through. If you are choosing to use your own pulses, you will need to soak them overnight.

🖋 If using the vegetable mixture, add the rice as soon as the water has come to the boil, and when the 50 minutes or so are up (or the pulses have begun to soften), add the frozen sweetcorn. Once the sweetcorn has cooked through, drain off the excess water and allow the 'Bean Soup' to cool.

🖋 Once cooled down, place in a tub or container and take out to the bird table. Any that is left over can be frozen.

Millet & Rice

This recipe is something of a 'winter warmer'. While it can be served up at almost any time of the year, it's best to avoid doing so in the middle of summer. Seed eaters such as Finches will enjoy this dish, as will Thrushes, especially if you add a little chopped apple to the mixture.

Ingredients

½ cup cooked de-husked millet (sweetcorn can be used as an alternative)

½ cup cooked white rice

½ cup cooked brown rice

Method

🕊 Soak the millet in water for around 30 minutes before you start to cook the mixture. Prepare the white and brown rice together as you would normally, and gently warm the millet through until soft.

🕊 Once you have cooked the millet and the two rices, mix them together. Then, while the mixture is still warm (but not hot), pop the 'Millet & Rice' out onto the bird table.

Popcorn Strings

Another winter favourite that is wonderfully simple to make. Almost every bird that visits the garden, from Sparrows to Waxeyes and other nimble birds, will find something tasty and nutritious for them on the end of 'Popcorn Strings'.

Ingredients

1 packet uncooked popcorn

1 jar malt (sunflower or olive oil will
do as an alternative)

1 cup wild bird seed

1 cup breadcrumbs

Method

✒ The joy of this recipe is the simplicity of it all. Simply cook your popcorn as per the instructions on the packet. Once the popcorn is ready, head towards the sewing box! Take a needle and some strong thread. Thread the needle, and begin to pass the thread through the freshly cooked popcorn. Make the 'Popcorn Strings' as long as you fancy and, if you wish, simply hang them up around the garden. As an alternative, you may want to add a little more colour and flavour to them first: brush on some warmed malt or some oil, and then roll the strings of popcorn in wild bird seed or breadcrumbs. You may want to chill the strings after that or hang them straight out in the garden.

✒ One final, colourful addition to the strings would be some soft fruit. If you have raspberries or blackberries in the freezer from the autumn, defrost a few and alternate fruit–popcorn–fruit–popcorn on your strings. Failing that, try some peeled oranges or apples – your local Waxeyes will be so grateful!

Breads & Buns, Pancakes & Peanut Butter

One of the staples of the human diet is bread. It's almost as popular with garden birds! While many of them enjoy nibbling on any breadcrumbs that you leave out for them, they are sure to enjoy the following recipes even more. As well as bread recipes, I've also included some recipes that use another bird recipe staple, unsalted peanut butter. This gives the birds a tremendous energy boost and the recipes are easy to do and fun too!

The Fabulous Flying Bird Bread I

This recipe and the next are adapted from ideas that have been a real boon for garden birds in America for decades and can work just as well here. The combination of ingredients will prove popular with many different species and provides perfect nourishment for garden visitors throughout the year.

Ingredients

2 cups baking mixture (any cake or pancake mixture will be sufficient)

2 cups white or yellow cornmeal (or crushed stale cornflakes/rice bubbles)

1 cup wholemeal flour

2 tablespoons baking powder

4 medium or 3 large eggs

3 small jars fruit purée or vegetable meals (as are suitable for babies) – alternatively, purée your own

Method

✈ Pre-heat your oven to around 190°C. As the oven is warming up, grease a large cake tin, around 23 x 30cm.

✈ Combine all of the dry ingredients in a bowl and then add the eggs and the jars of fruit purée and vegetables. Stir the mixture well until all the dry ingredients are nicely moistened. By this time the mixture will be very heavy and thick. Now pour the mixture into the cake tin.

✈ Bake the bread for around 40 minutes, or until the top has become golden brown and fairly hard. Once the loaf is cooked, allow it to cool completely before you cut it into cubes ready for the bird table or your bird feeders. Keep enough cubes aside for a few days' feeding and freeze the remainder to use as and when you please.

✈ The recipe can be modified to include almost anything that you fancy using. Anything from chopped fruit and vegetables to unsalted peanut butter and cheese will work perfectly well within the 'The Fabulous Flying Bird Bread I'.

The Fabulous Flying Bird Bread II

Another great bird bread recipe and, again, one that is pretty simple to put together. Use the cornbread mixture from page 22 for a different treat for the birds. The blend of ingredients will prove popular with many species that visit the garden.

Ingredients

1 quantity cornbread mix (page 22)

1 extra egg (i.e. one extra to the amount needed for the cornbread)

Fruit juice of your choice

½ cup de-husked raw sunflower seeds (available in supermarkets, as well as wholefood shops)

1 cup fresh chopped vegetable of your choice

1 cup fresh chopped fruit of your choice

½ cup raisins

½ cup de-husked raw millet seed (available in wholefood shops)

Method

✒ Pre-heat your oven to around 190°C. As the oven is warming up, grease a large cake tin, around 23 x 30cm.

✒ Make up the cornbread mixture as set out on page 22. You may need to substitute some of the liquid used in the recipe, as you will be adding fruit juice, and another egg.

✒ Once the eggs and fruit juice are combined, add in the sunflower seeds, the vegetable and the fruit. Mix together well before adding the raisins. Mix well, then pour into the cake tin. Before you put it into the oven, sprinkle with the millet seed.

✒ Bake the bread until golden brown and hard on the crust. Check with a toothpick that the centre is baked. Once the loaf has cooled, cut it into cubes and place some crumbled cubes onto the bird table, or into a bird food holder. Any leftovers can be frozen and used as you wish.

✒ You can use cooked pasta or beans instead of vegetables. Unsalted peanut butter or apple sauce can also be used (if you use either, reduce the liquid accordingly).

The King's Bread Pudding

One of my very favourite recipes to make, and one that the birds seem to love, this is a winter recipe, named in tribute to the similarly fearsome snack of choice that 'The King' enjoyed so much in his later years. This is crammed full of flavoursome items that all manner of garden birds will keep coming back to!

Ingredients

1 large, fairly stale, unsliced bread loaf

1 jar unsalted peanut butter

1 cup unsalted peanuts

½ cup sunflower seeds

1 cup raisins

½ cup diced apple

½ cup sweetcorn

Method

🔪 Cut the crust off one end of the bread (break it up and pop out onto the bird table). Then, with your hands, or a spoon, hollow out the inside of the loaf as much as you can. (Scatter these breadcrumbs onto the bird table too.)

🔪 Once the bread is hollowed out, use a skewer to make two holes in the other end of the loaf, through the end crust, keeping the holes as far apart as possible. Thread some strong string or twine (even thin rope) through the two holes, first passing it *out* of the loaf from inside, then back *into* the loaf via the second hole.

🔪 Fill the loaf cavity with a mixture of the other ingredients, making sure that you're generous with the peanut butter. Once the loaf is full to the brim, you can hang it up in the garden. You may want to experiment with 'perches' for the birds within the loaf. Funnily enough, cream crackers on the top may work, but they aren't so successful on the side. It's a case of trial and error to find what works best!

Peanut Butter Balls

As with lots of other recipes in the book, this one is quick and easy to make, and the birds really do seem to enjoy the combination of unsalted peanut butter, cereal, nuts and fruit. If it wasn't for the lard, you might be tempted to have one too! Your local Waxeyes and Sparrows will enjoy them.

Ingredients

1½ cups lard

1½ cups unsalted crunchy peanut butter

5 cups crushed stale cornflakes/rice bubbles (or cornmeal)

1 cup chopped mixed nuts

½ cup chopped dried fruit

Method

🖋 Melt the lard slowly in a saucepan over a gentle heat. Once the lard has melted completely, start to add in the peanut butter, stirring until it has combined well with the lard. Add in the crushed cornflakes/rice bubbles and, once the cereal has been absorbed into the mixture, drop in the mixed nuts and finally the dried fruit. If the mixture is still a bit runny, add in some more cornflakes/rice crispies to stiffen things up a little.

🖋 Allow the mixture to harden in the fridge. You can then put it into a sturdy mesh bag or, preferably, into a square mesh feeder.

Rock Cakes

This is such a simple garden bird snack to make! It's almost identical to the traditional just-like-granny-used-to-make recipe, and little effort is required to create the finished product. A nice, crumbly, fruit-laden cake appears at the end of the cooking process and will be devoured by Waxeyes, Starlings, Sparrows and more besides. These 'Rock Cakes' can be put out directly onto a bird table, or suspended in a wire mesh holder.

Ingredients

1 large tub margarine – around 225g

1kg self-raising flour

A little water

4 tbsp sugar

2–3 generous handfuls raisins and currants

Method

✒ Pre-heat your oven to a moderate temperature – around 180°C should do it. As the oven warms up, grease a large cake tin, or a couple of bun trays, ready for the simple mixture.

✒ Before combining the ingredients, make sure that the margarine is softened first as (just like cooking for yourself) this will help speed up the process when blending the ingredients. Once the margarine is nice and soft, add the flour (sift it if you have the time). Add a little water at this point to help to bind the mixture. Next add the sugar and fruit, mix well and again add a little water to bind if required.

✒ Pour the mixture into your cake tin or bun trays and bake until the crust of the 'Rock Cake' is golden brown and firm to the touch. Once cooled, pop out as much as you want onto the bird table. The rest can be frozen for another time.

Pancake Treats

Don't wait for Shrove Tuesday; these can be made any time. If you keep chooks and have a surplus of eggs, here is one way to use some up. With all the fruit, the Blackbirds and Thrushes will love this meal.

Ingredients

2 eggs

2 cups self-raising flour

1 heaped teaspoon baking powder

300ml liquid (half milk, half water)

1 cup chopped mixed nuts

1 cup raisins (or mixed fruit)

1 cup chopped dried fruits (fresh fruits may also be added,
like banana, apple or pear)

Method

✒ Why not make the birds their very own batch of pancakes? Make the pancakes as you would make them for yourself. Heat pan with a little oil and pour in the batter mixture.

✒ Once the pancakes are in the pan and the batter is still cooking, add in a handful or two of your chosen topping, be it nuts or fruit. Continue to cook the pancakes as normal, turning once.

✒ Allow the pancakes to cool down, then tear them up and pop them outside and onto the bird table.

✒ Any leftover pancakes can be stored in the freezer, but remember to place a sheet of greaseproof paper between them to help separate them.

Pancake Bird Bars

As if tempting you with one pancake recipe isn't enough, here comes another! Actually the end product is far less appetising to our eyes – more a bird bar than a pancake – but as pancake mixture is the core ingredient it's allowed the grand 'Pancake Bird Bars' title. Almost every species in the garden will take a nibble at these wholesome snacks.

Ingredients

2 eggs

1 cup wild bird seed

1 large carrot

½ cup fresh raw broccoli

⅓ cup mixed nuts (not peanuts and not salted)

1 quantity pancake mix from page 44

1 jar kumara and sweetcorn mash (or similar) baby food, or purée your own

1 jar potatoes, peas and broccoli (or similar) baby food, or, again, purée your own

Method

🔸 Pre-heat your oven to around 190°C and grease a large baking tray. As the oven is heating, mix the following ingredients in a blender: the eggs (including shells), wild bird seed, vegetables and nuts. Whizz them through at high speed until everything is well and truly mashed and puréed.

🔸 Drop the pancake mixture into a large mixing bowl. Pour in the purée of egg, vegetables and nuts, followed by the baby food. With a sizeable spoon, stir the mixture until everything is blended well (this may take several minutes) and is fairly smooth in consistency (though it should remain sticky and a bit lumpy). If it seems to be a little on the thick side, add a little water.

🔸 Pour or spoon the mixture onto the baking tray and put it into the oven. Bake for around 30 minutes, until golden brown. Ensure the mixture is cooked through.

🔸 Allow the cake to cool for a few minutes, but while still warm, cut it into bars. Put the bars out immediately, freezing any that are left over for another time.

Breakfast Bagels

It's not just people who enjoy taking their place at the dining table to nibble on a breakfast bagel. Think of all those species that squabble over the breadcrumbs that you put out for them – the Starlings, Blackbirds and Sparrows. All of these species and a few more besides will enjoy this quick and easy bready treat.

Ingredients

1 pack plain bagels

Malt

Several generous handfuls wild bird seed

Method

🐦 Prepare the bagels as you would if you were warming them through for yourself. Once they are ready, split the bagels open and pour or spread on the malt.

🐦 Once sufficient malt is oozing into the bagel, simply cover each half with wild bird seed (the malt should ensure that a lot sticks) and pop them out into suspended wire mesh feeders.

Bird Bread Pudding

Bird food recipes are, as often as not, successful variations on a theme. This recipe certainly follows in the footsteps of other bread pudding recipes that have come and gone in the cooking-for-birds history books. Simple to do and undoubtedly a big hit with many garden bird visitors.

Ingredients

Approx. 800g lard or margarine

3 heaped cups porridge oats

1 heaped cup currants (or raisins)

Good handful grated cheese

Good handful wild bird seed

Method

🖋 Gently melt down the lard or margarine over a medium heat. Once the fat has melted, gradually mix in the oats, followed by the currants, cheese and wild bird seed. Combine the ingredients well, then spoon out into any suitable containers that you have spare (margarine tubs are ideal). Alternatively, form them into shapes that will fit into your sturdy string bag or wire mesh feeders.

🖋 Once the 'Bird Bread Pudding' mixture is in place in containers, put them into the fridge, allowing them to set and firm up before serving them up on the bird table.

Sweet & Fruity

Many birds love to feed on fruit. Barely an autumn or winter goes by when windfall apples aren't being devoured by local Blackbirds. Try your luck with Tui, too, who may just drop in to feast on your fruit offerings. As well as cutting up various fruits – from apples to oranges, plums to nectarines – try some of your local birds out on some raw veggies, too. Broccoli, tomatoes and green peppers appear to be popular here. Do be careful in warm, summer weather – try to ensure that the fruit and veg stays mould-free and doesn't spoil. Always cut and peel the fruit so the birds do not associate the food with what is grown on your trees, otherwise they will raid your trees.

Fruity Ice

Here's a slightly wacky recipe for the summertime. See how the garden bird visitors fare with this stunningly simple treat. The Thrushes should enjoy it, and it is doubtful that any other species would get a look in!

Ingredients

As many types of fresh fruit as are available

Method

- Take all your fruits and dice them into medium-sized chunks. Toss them into a food processor and mash them until smooth and thoroughly mixed.

- Once the fruit is nicely puréed, put the liquid into ice cube trays (or ice cube bags if you prefer) and freeze until totally solid.

- Use the cubes as and when you think the birds will fancy them. They should prove to be a funky summertime alternative!

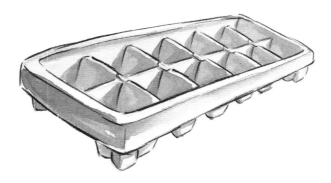

Lollipop, Lollipop!

It has long been known that caged birds have something of a penchant for nibbling, chewing and licking sweet treats, but this is also the case for wild birds, too. Here's a recipe similar to 'Malt Twigs', but with a little more on offer for the more discerning garden bird visitor!

Ingredients

Lollipop sticks	½ cup chopped nuts
½ cup mixed dried fruit	1 egg
½ cup wild bird seed	Some warmed malt

Method

✎ Pre-heat your oven to around 35°C. Arrange the lollipop sticks on a baking tray and put them in the oven, just to warm them

✎ As the sticks are gently warming through, put the nuts, fruits and bird seed into a mixing bowl. Crack the egg (discarding the shells) and bind all the ingredients together, until everything is nice and sticky!

✎ Remove the heated lollipop sticks from the oven and turn the heat up to around 70°C. While the sticks are still warm (but not too hot), start to form the lollipops. Grab a small handful of the mixture and form it into a ball around the stick. You can, of course, vary the size of the lollipops.

✎ Put the newly formed lollipops back into the hot oven on the baking tray and bake for 20–30 minutes. Once they appear nicely toasted, then they are done.

✎ Take the toasted lollipops from the oven and coat the whole of the lollipop and the stick with malt. Then return them to the oven for around 5 minutes.

✎ Allow the lollipops to cool completely before putting them out into the garden. You can hang them up or insert them into bird feeders that may already be hanging in the garden. Any leftover lollipops can be stored in an airtight container for several days.

Funky Alfresco Fruit Salad

Here's another summertime recipe to give the hard-working bird parents a little treat. No cooking is required and you can prepare this colourful and nutritious dish in a matter of minutes.

Ingredients

2 medium-sized oranges

1 small banana

1 cup strawberries

Small bunch seedless grapes
(around 30 or so)

1 small apple

Method

- Prepare your fruit. Peel the oranges, peel and slice the banana and cut the strawberries in half. You may want to cut the grapes in half, too. Cut and dice the apple.

- Once the fruits are cut and sliced, all that remains to be done is to combine the ingredients in a bowl and mix them well. And that's it! Put the fruit mixture into a bird bowl and out onto the bird table. Any remaining fruit salad can be frozen.

Corn-on-the-cob – With a Twist!

The best thing with any recipe, whether cooking is involved or not, is simplicity. Many of the recipes within the book are deliberately simple, and this idea is as simple as they come. All you need are some corn-on-the-cobs and some fruit. Hopefully, within no time at all, a variety of species, from Blackbirds to Thrushes, Waxeyes and Sparrows, will be investigating this colourful meal.

Ingredients

1 fresh ear corn-on-the-cob (still in its husk)

Small selection of seasonal fruit

Skewers, corks (to ensure that no sharp skewer points injure the birds),
and strong string or twine

Method

✎ Carefully remove the husk and the silk-like strings from the corn. Gently push the skewer through the cob and then, at either end, pop on some chunks of fruit, prior to hanging. Using the twine, tie the fruit-laden corn cob onto an overhanging branch or onto a sturdy feeding station.

✎ Alternatively, you can keep the fruit and the vegetable separately, and hang the corn on its own and use the skewers solely for fruit.

Fruitcake-come-cupcake

Everyone loves fruitcake, even the garden birds, who will all be jostling for a slice of the action when stale, dry fruitcake is put out onto the bird table. But instead of using the stale remnants, how about spending some time preparing the birds their very own 'Fruitcake-come-cupcake'?

Ingredients

2–3 kumara (or jars of vegetable baby food)

Summer fruits of your choice, stewed and puréed

3 eggs

1½ cups wild bird seed

Method

✎ Prepare and cook your kumara as you would normally. For speed, you may choose to cook it for around 20 minutes or so, until it is soft enough to mash.

✎ Once the kumara is soft enough to mash, pop it into a food processor and purée – there shouldn't be any need to add any liquid to this purée. Then put the fruit into the food processor and blend together. Pre-heat the oven to 200°C.

✎ Add the eggs (including shells) to the kumara and fruit purée. Whizz the food processor again, until the shells are totally blended into the mixture. Once the eggs have been blended, add in the wild bird seed and blend again for a few seconds, until you have a smooth mixture.

✎ Grease a bun tray and then pour about a quarter of a cup of the mixture into the individual compartments on the tray. Place the tray into the oven and cook for around 15–20 minutes, or until 'Fruitcake-come-cupcake' is firm to the touch.

✎ Once cooked, allow the cakes to cool down completely before putting them out for the birds.

Blueberry Butter Balls

Quick and easy, here is another 'no need for the oven' recipe, guaranteed to be a draw to those species that love both fruit and seeds … and peanut butter!

Ingredients

7 cups plain cooked popcorn

Handful unsalted peanuts
(out of their skins)

Handful sunflower seeds (in husks)

Handful crushed stale
cornflakes/rice crispies

1 jar unsalted crunchy
peanut butter

1 cup raisins

1 cup blueberries

1 cup blackberries

Method

✎ Cook the popcorn, ensuring you have enough to fill around seven cups. After that, let the mixing begin!

✎ Put all the ingredients into a large bowl, apart from the berries, and combine with the peanut butter and the popcorn, until everything is well coated. At the last minute add in the berries. Try to keep the soft fruit as whole as you can.

✎ Put the mixture into some tough mesh bags and chill them (to help them set) before hanging them out in the garden.

The Pleasure of Pasta!

The great thing about this recipe is that you don't have to cook the core ingredient especially for the occasion. All you need to do is ensure that, whenever you cook spaghetti, penne, rigatoni or macaroni, you make extra! Given the starchy nature of the main ingredient, this is perhaps one of those winter-only recipes, giving the birds a little carbohydrate boost on a chilly day.

Ingredients

Sunflower, vegetable or olive oil

Raisins

Pasta (dried or fresh)

Fruit of your choice (fresh or tinned)

Method

✒ Prepare your pasta as per the cooking instructions on the packet.
If you are using spaghetti, try to remember to break it into smaller
pieces before cooking.

✒ While the pasta is cooking, grab a couple of handfuls of raisins and soak
them in warm water so that they 'puff up' a little. Drain them after a few
minutes and they should look suitably juicy.

✒ Once the pasta is cooked, drain and then add sufficient oil to thinly coat
the pasta. Add in the raisins and any fruits you wish to include – apples are always
a good option. Remember to cut the fruit into small pieces and to drain any juice
from tinned fruit.

✒ Allow the mixture to cool, then pop it onto the bird table or into a suitable
sturdy feeder.

✒ As an alternative, you can use unsalted peanut butter instead of oil, with raisins
and fruits as an optional extra.

Simply Sugar Water!

This is one of the easiest recipes in the book, but it's sure to attract nectar-loving Tui to your garden. If you have Tui regularly visiting, there'll be a good chance they will respond to food placed in a tree they frequent.

Ingredients
(for a 15 per cent concentration)

3 dessertspoons white sugar

1 cup water

1–3 teaspoons vanilla Complan
(a dietary supplement powder)

Method

⚟ Mix the water and sugar together in a bowl. The bowl should have a wide edge (wider than 1cm) so that Tui can perch on the side. A longer, trough-like feeding bowl works best, as it allows more than one Tui to feed at a time.

⚟ Add 1–2 teaspoons of vanilla Complan. Stir well so the sugar and Complan dissolve. The concentration of sugar is important. You can start off with up to 50 per cent of sugar to get Tui interested, but once Tui become regular tea-time guests, drop the concentration of sugar to no more than 15 per cent. Otherwise, Tui might be tempted away from the natural nectar provided by flowers.

⚟ Make sure the sugar water is changed regularly and the feeding bowl is cleaned properly.

Super Squidgy Suet

Many birds love suet, but remember that suet (and lard) are both animal products, and those people who are vegetarian with a love of birds might prefer not to handle animal products. As an excellent substitute, and recipe alternative, you can use vegetable suet or vegetable shortening, both of which are easily found in almost every supermarket these days.

A Few Words About Suet ...

Before going any further, it might be useful to explain what is meant by 'suet' and 'lard'. In terms of feeding birds, the word 'suet' has come to mean any generally fatty meal, but there is actually a specific fat type called suet – this being the fat found around a cow's or lamb's kidney. The word 'lard' used to apply just to pork fat, but is used in bird food recipe terms to refer to any animal fat.

Vegetable shortening (and suet) was first launched in America as long ago as 1912. Popular in the home because it lasted far longer than animal fat, vegetable shortening is, basically, 'fats' from vegetables, which can be used in cooking. Vegetable shortening lasts far longer in warm conditions than any kind of animal fat, which should be borne in mind when feeding garden birds.

Many species are very partial to food items that have suet as a major ingredient. Waxeyes and Starlings are species that thrive on suety recipes, but other species, such as Blackbirds, Thrushes and Sparrows, will also be more than happy to feed on suet-based foods. The energy source that suet provides is invaluable to birds, particularly during winter months and spells of cold weather. Many species burn energy at an amazing rate, particularly in very cold conditions, or when they are especially active in the build-up to the breeding season.

To help birds as best you can, try to ensure that the species visiting your garden can feed on something that is both high in energy (i.e. high in fat) and easy to digest. Note that because of its chemical composition, lard is about twice as hard to digest as vegetable shortening and birds will gain more energy out of vegetable shortening than they will from animal fat. Vegetable shortening and vegetable suet are also healthier for garden birds because they contain around half the saturated fatty acids of animal suet and lard. The vegetable-based fats also contain more vitamins and essential nutrients, while lard has only trace amounts of them.

However, this should not detract from the use animal fats have in the feeding of garden birds. A visit to the local butcher for some real suet of the beef kidney type will provide birds with a massive energy boost from its high fat and protein content. Given the problems of animal fats going off in warm weather, it may be best to use this as a treat only in winter.

Within this section, a number of the recipes featured make use of the now-familiar square mesh plastic-coated metal cages, which are readily found in shops that sell wild bird foodstuffs. As an alternative, you can try using a small string bag, but these really aren't up to the job, as they tear easily and perhaps last just one or two visits.

Simply Suet

This is a very simple, very quick recipe that should see instant results when hung in a feeder or container. Almost every species of garden bird will find something in the recipe to excite them!

Ingredients

1½ cups melted suet (animal or vegetable)

1½ cups brown breadcrumbs (white breadcrumbs are fine too)

¼ cup granulated sugar

2 tablespoons unsalted crunchy peanut butter

1 cup porridge oats

½ cup plain flour

½ cup wild bird seed

Method

✦ After melting the suet, simply mix all of the ingredients together in a large saucepan over a fairly low heat. Keep stirring until all the ingredients are thoroughly mixed together.

✦ When you are happy that everything is blended well, start to spoon, or pour, the mixture into your chosen containers (sturdy paper cups are really good for this) and let them cool down until hard. Before spooning the mixture in, make a hole in the middle of the base of the cup and thread a piece of strong string through, with a knot in the end of it, and pour the mixture around the knotted string.

✦ Once nice and hard, take the cup away, leaving the string in place to tie around small branches. Alternatively, place slabs of the mixture into your feeders.

Simply Suet – A Veggie Version

This recipe uses only vegetable suet/shortening as one of its main ingredients. Many of the suet recipes included in the book are suitable for using either animal or vegetable suets. Obviously, if you wish to, you can use animal fat here, but the birds seem to like it as it is.

Ingredients

1 cup vegetable suet or shortening

1 cup unsalted peanut butter

½ cup shelled unsalted peanuts

½ cup raisins

½ cup cornmeal (or crushed stale cornflakes/rice bubbles)

½ cup maize/sweetcorn/cracked corn (use whichever you can find!)

Method

✒ Take the vegetable suet and melt it down in a large saucepan over a gentle heat. Once this is done, add in the peanut butter and allow that to melt into the suet mixture. Once the two are blended together, slowly add in the remaining ingredients, one at a time. Mix them together well until everything has stuck together (yes, it is that simple!). Spoon the ingredients into a container (a baking tray, or paper cups with added string for tying to a branch) and allow them to harden. You may wish to chill, or even freeze, them briefly.

✒ You can add anything to this (and many other recipes), with small apple chunks or wild bird seed always proving extra popular.

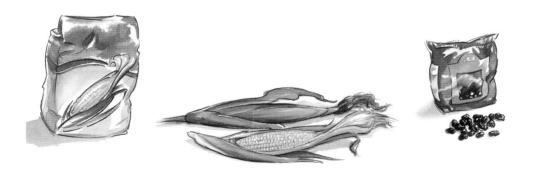

Chewy Bird Bars!

Well, these aren't really chewy bars, but they certainly resemble the chewy cereal-based bars that are available in most shops. The recipe comes in two stages and is certain to please many species, particularly Chaffinches and, if you are lucky, perhaps some native birds.

Ingredients

½ cup suet (animal or vegetable)

½ cup unsalted peanut butter (crunchy is best)

2½ cups cornmeal (or crushed stale cornflakes/rice bubbles)

1 cup wild bird seed

Additional suet

¼ cup unsalted peanuts

½ cup raisins

1 apple, chopped

Method

✍ Melt down the suet, then add the peanut butter, cornmeal/cornflakes/rice bubbles and seeds. Mix thoroughly on a low to moderate heat and press out onto an old baking tray. Place the tray into the freezer compartment until the 'Chewy Bird Bar' mixture is firm enough for you to crumble. When it reaches this stage, crumble the whole batch and place it into a large mixing bowl.

✍ Add more suet, along with the peanuts, raisins and chopped apple. If you feel that more fat is needed for binding the mixture, then add some. There's no exact science to this recipe!

✍ When the ingredients are well mixed for the second time, fill your containers (the mesh feeding 'cage' or paper cups are fine) and freeze them until required.

Chunky Seed Balls

The following three recipes have proved very popular with the visitors to many gardens. This first recipe is an adaptation of 'Chewy Bird Bars', without the addition of fruit, something that some species appear to appreciate.

Ingredients

3 cups suet (animal or vegetable)

1½ cups unsalted crunchy peanut butter

1½ cups crushed stale cornflakes/ rice bubbles (or cornmeal, if available)

3–4 cups wild bird seed

Method

✎ Melt the suet gently in a large pan over a low heat. Once the suet has turned to liquid, add the peanut butter, cornflakes/rice bubbles/cornmeal and bird seeds. When the ingredients have been mixed well, turn the mixture out into an old baking tray or cake tin, cut into sizeable chunks and freeze them until required.

✎ As an alternative when using animal suet, you may wish to render it before mixing with the other ingredients. To do this, melt it over a very low heat and allow to cool before repeating the process. While in its melted state, add the additional ingredients.

Sweet Peanut Treats

Another devilishly quick and simple recipe for a popular bird snack.

The high fat content of the lard will appeal to many birds, while

the sweetness provided by the sugar is sure to be a hit with Thrushes,

Finches and Waxeyes.

Ingredients

1 cup lard (no substitutions allowed here!)

1 cup unsalted crunchy peanut butter

2 cups porridge oats (the quick-cooking microwave type)

2 cups cornmeal (or crushed stale cornflakes/rice bubbles)

1 cup plain flour

¼ cup granulated sugar

Method

✒ In a saucepan, melt the lard and peanut butter together over a low heat. Once you have a suitably gloopy mixture, add the other ingredients in turn, stirring frequently. When you are happy that the ingredients have been mixed together sufficiently, pour out into a baking tray to around 2.5–5cm in depth.

✒ Pop the baking tray into the freezer and cut out blocks from there as and when they are required.

Nutty Oatcakes

The final recipe of this trio – using the staples of suet, unsalted peanut butter and oats – is another fantastically simple recipe to put together and an ideal one in which to involve the children. It's popular with almost every visitor to the garden, especially Finches and Thrushes.

Ingredients

1 cup animal suet or lard (or use vegetable suet if you'd prefer)

1 cup unsalted crunchy peanut butter

2 cups porridge oats (preferably the quick-cooking microwave type)

2 cups cornmeal (or crushed stale cornflakes/rice bubbles)

1 cup plain flour

1 cup wild bird seed

Method

★ In a large saucepan, melt the fat along with the peanut butter over a low heat. Once you are happy that they are fully mixed, add in the dry ingredients one at a time. When all the ingredients are thoroughly mixed, take a margarine tub and half fill it before freezing.

★ If you want to re-use the tub after freezing, simply ease the frozen food block out of the tub, wrap it and put it back in the freezer.

★ When using the blocks, allow them to defrost before hanging them in the garden.

Pinecone Pleaser

Pinecones have a wonderful natural shape that just cries out to be utilised as a bird feeder! This recipe is a quick, simple way of providing nourishment for your garden birds. Next time you are out walking, find the largest pinecones you can (or cones from a large banksia tree), and rustle up a pan of 'Pinecone Pleaser'.

Ingredients

4½ cups suet (animal or vegetable)

1 cup dried, crumbled bread (wholemeal is best)

½ cup shelled sunflower seeds

¼ cup millet seeds

¼ cup raisins (or, alternatively, chopped dried apples)

Pinecones (fully opened)

Method

✎ Melt your suet over a low heat in a saucepan. If you choose to use animal suet for this recipe, you may wish to render it first. Once the suet has melted, leave it to one side to cool down a little. While it is cooling, take a large mixing bowl and mix together the remaining ingredients (apart from the pine cones), stirring well.

✎ Once the cooling suet begins to thicken slightly, gradually stir it into the remaining ingredients, mixing them all thoroughly.

✎ Now for the pinecones! Stuff the mixture between the hard 'leaves' or 'petals' of the cone. Once the cones are full to the brim, hang them in the garden and enjoy the results.

Muffintastic!

It's those core suet and peanut butter ingredients again, but they prove almost irresistible to so many garden species. The suggestion is to hang them up in your bird feeders, but you can just as easily use them by crumbling the muffins up and putting them out onto the bird table. This is a variation on a theme, but a little variety in the recipe and presentation department seems to be as appreciated by the birds as it is by us!

Ingredients

1 cup suet (animal or vegetable)

1 cup unsalted peanut butter (smooth or crunchy)

3 cups porridge oats or cornmeal

½ cup wholemeal flour

Method

✎ Put your cup of suet into a saucepan and melt slowly over a low heat. Gently stir in the peanut butter until well blended together. Once this is done, allow the suet/peanut butter mixture to cool until it begins to thicken. While this happens, blend the dry ingredients together and, once the suet/peanut butter has thickened, combine it with the dry ingredients.

✎ Pour the mixture into a bun tray (or muffin tin, if you prefer) and freeze it. Use the buns as needed by hanging them in mesh food holders or putting them straight onto the bird table. As a gooey alternative, you could try and smear the non-frozen mixture on a tree trunk. You never know your luck!

✎ The bun/muffin mixture can also be supplemented with raisins and breadcrumbs.

Black Treacle Balls

Part of the pleasure in cooking for birds is to see the results of your labours meet with a resounding 'thumbs up' from the garden visitors that you are catering for. Here is another 'bird balls' type of recipe that combines many familiar ingredients into a gooey sticky mess!

Ingredients

2 cups stale breadcrumbs

¼ cup cornmeal (or crushed stale cornflakes/rice bubbles)

½ cup flour (wholewheat if possible)

½ cup sugar

4 apples, chopped into small pieces

1 cup raisins

1 cup wild bird seed

1 cup unsalted peanuts

½ cup grated cheese

1 cup suet

¾ of a jar unsalted crunchy peanut butter

1–2 spoonfuls black treacle

Method

✎ This is another recipe where all you have to do is mix everything in together! It's great fun when it's as easy as this.

✎ Combine the first nine ingredients.

✎ Add the suet, peanut butter and black treacle. (The treacle is used to assist the binding process as much as anything else.)

✎ Once all the ingredients are well combined, you should be left with a fairly firm, yet still gooey, mixture. If the mixture is still a little on the dry side, you can add in a little more suet to bind ingredients together.

✎ Shape this mixture into balls and leave them in the fridge to set. Place the chilled balls into a tough mesh bag and hang them up in trees, bushes or from the bird table. Additional balls can be frozen until you need them.

Further Reading

You may need to scout around second-hand bookshops for one or two of these books, but they're well worth making the effort for the first-rate information they contain.

Ell, Gordon, **Enjoying Nature in the New Zealand Garden**
(The Bush Press, 1995)

Gill, Brian, and Moon, Geoff, **New Zealand's Unique Birds**
(Reed Publishing (NZ) Ltd, 1999)

Hayman, Piers, **The Bird Next Door**
(New Holland (NZ) Ltd, 1999)

Heather, Barrie, and Robertson, Hugh, **Field Guide to the Birds of New Zealand**
(Penguin Books (NZ) Ltd, 2005)

Hunt, Janet, **A Bird in the Hand: Keeping New Zealand Wildlife Safe**
(Random House New Zealand Ltd, 2004)

Moon, Geoff, **A Photographic Guide to Birds of New Zealand**
(New Holland (NZ) Ltd, 2002)

Moon, Lynnette, and Moon, Geoff, **Know Your New Zealand Birds**
(New Holland (NZ) Ltd, 2006

Morris, Rod, and Smith, Hal, **Saving New Zealand's Endangered Birds**
(TVNZ/Random House New Zealand Ltd, 1995)

Useful Addresses

Department of Conservation
Website: www.doc.govt.nz

Forest and Bird Protection Society
Wellington Central Office
Level One, 90 Ghuznee Street
PO Box 631
Wellington, New Zealand
Phone: (04) 385 7374
Freephone for membership enquiries:
0800 200 064
Email:office@forestandbird.org.nz
Website: www.forestandbird.org.nz

Kiwi Conservation Club
*Contact details as for Forest and Bird
Protection Society*
The Kiwi Conservation Club is a Forest and
Bird project for children

New Zealand Birds
Website: www.nzbirds.com

**The Ornithological Society of
New Zealand**
PO Box 12397
Wellington, New Zealand
Email: OSNZ@xtra.co.nz
Website: www.osnz.org.nz

Whakatane Bird Rescue
The author's own bird rescue initiative,
based in Whakatane, Bay of Plenty.
Email: rosemarytully@clear.net.nz
Website: www.nzbirds.com/more/
rescue.html

What Bird?
Website: www.whatbird.co.nz

Index